Poems by Christine

CHRISTINE BRYANT

Unless otherwise indicated, all scripture references are from the King James Version of the Bible.

Poems by Christine
ISBN 978-0-578-93312-2
Copyright © 2020

Proofread and Edited by: Dagny Griffin
Text Design: Greg Lane, Inspired Design & Graphics
Cover Design: Greg Lane, Inspired Design & Graphics

Contents

Introduction

I began enjoying poetry as a little girl reading Dr. Seuss books. Poetry fascinated me, especially the rhyming. At some point during my adult life, I began to write some poetry as I was inspired. The poems I wrote were for others or myself. I had never intended to put them in a book for publishing.

One day, it seemed as if God was instructing me to publish the poems in a book. This was shocking to me. As stated in the previous paragraph, I had never intended to publish them. I guess it had become a hobby for me to just dabble in from time to time. I also hadn't written very many, so the book wouldn't be big at all. However, I was quickly reminded that what we view as small may not be small to someone else, including God. Maybe He saw the poems as being a blessing and a help to those who read them.

All the poems I've written as an adult (minus two) are enclosed. One is already in my book Delivered From Misery. Due to certain copyright rules, I could't put that poem in this book. The other one is an old love song I decided to rewrite to God. I couldn't put that one in here due to copyright rules as well.

I certainly hope the poems enclosed will be enjoyed. May they be an inspiration to many.

My Grandmother
(whom we affectionately called Nanny)

When you were rushed to the hospital, I thought it was time
To let you go and say goodbye.
We started a phone chain alerting all members
That you were not well; Our Nanny, so precious, so tender.
All of our hearts sank one by one
As we heard the terrible news that Nanny was gone
To the emergency room as sick as can be
That was something we NEVER did see.
You have been around to care for 3 generations
Of your children, grand-children, and even the great ones.
You have always been there to take care of us all
While we were sick, hungry, or just had a bad fall.
We're all glad that you are still here
Most don't want to let go but continue to keep you near.
However, we all know
that whenever the time does come we must let go!
Now I can see how selfish and unfair it is
To want to keep someone here when their life they have lived
To the fullest and to a ripe age
I know it will hurt but we must turn the page.
I can't bring myself to see you right now.
Someone called me a chicken but I don't know how
To let go of the memories I have of you
And replace them with seeing you down.
I can't, I'm used to seeing you up and around.

July 18, 2004

7

Freedom

I don't remember what I did with the rest.
I do know it was wisely spent by one of the best
Because the Lord Jesus Christ helps me in all I do
I don't have to worry like I used to.

However, I still need to keep accurate track
Of where the money went so I won't go lack
In my records I refer to so often back to back.

I'm lovin' this freedom and peace of mind
Peace and freedom with money, spirit, and time,
Also, peace and freedom with space
In my lovely new place.

The Lord has blessed me tremendously
And will continue – for it was prophesied to me
"My latter life will be greater than my former"
You'll see.

August 27, 2009

A Place To Go

I prayed, pondered and worried constantly
About a place to go and worship in peace.
A place where the pastor would be true and sincere
Dedication to You would be obviously clear.
I desired a place to be fed Your Word properly
With my spiritual well being, everyone can't be trusted, you see
Souls are precious and must be cared for
In order to make it into heaven's door.
So I prayed and pondered, pondered and prayed
But Your master plan had already been put into play.
My former pastor, knowing my current one
And wanting me to meet him as well
So off to one Sunday morning service we went
And to my surprise, after one service I could tell
THAT THIS WAS THE PLACE!
My heart was attached after one visit
I no longer had to ponder or worry myself sick.
You so beautifully orchestrated this bond
That can never be broken
until it's Your time for me to move on.
The praise and worship service, led by the pastor's wife,
Was so anointed and filled with Your presence
That it alone could begin to give someone life.
And the way You've given this pastor to deliver Your word
Is so awesome because many I've heard

Don't rightly divide, being full of folly
But this pastor and wife are truly godly.
Together they serve You, fully allowing
You to guide them with a faithful following
Of others who are also hungry to hear
Your Word rightly divided to their spiritual ears.
THANK YOU LORD for proving to me once again
That You've got this – my life is in Your hands.

June 2010

Birthday
Poem to D.J.

My son, my son

This is my son, my first born, my oldest child
By first appearance, some think that he's wild.
But he's not, he's highly intelligent
Two degrees from Florida State he did get.
Still up in T-town doing his own thing
To earn paper and maybe get some bling-bling.
We love you D.J. and miss you very much
But God loves you best and I pray you will be touched
by Him.

January 28, 2011

MOM

You're the BEST mom a child could ever have.
You always took great care of us
And amazingly, without much fuss.
I don't remember you yelling like most parents do,
But it wasn't because we were great children to you.
It was because the love of Almighty God
Was already in your heart
Causing the light He placed in you
To shine bright in every part
Of your life.
You've always been calm, kind, and filled with joy
Until those pennies I received from that little boy.
A great lesson you taught me as I returned them to him with tears,
Yes, a lesson that's remained with me all these years!
You didn't even yell when I dirtied my hair and Easter dress.
Upset you were, but you just cleaned me and my mess.
There's so many wonderful things we can all say
About you on this, YOUR special day.
One poem can't contain it all
So I'll just leave it very small.

HAPPY BIRTHDAY MOM! I LOVE YOU!

March 21, 2013

Freedom #2

The first Freedom poem was about money and time
This poem is about freedom of a different kind.
I remember the days of not being fully free
To spend quality time with God in quantity and quality.
Though I loved being a wife and mother of four
Most of my time went to them and my job
Without much time left for God, who is my Core.
To the living room or bathroom sometimes I would sneak
In the middle of the night when I couldn't sleep.
The majority of those times were spent praying and singing
instead of reading
His word which was also heavily needed.
He blessed me with His presence and strengthened
me constantly
To continue working and taking excellent care of my
beautiful family.
And now since I'm divorced and all four children are grown,
I've had FREEDOM to spend more time with God
Since I am on my own.
And it feels great!
To the bathroom or living room I no longer have to sneak
In the middle of the night when awakened from my sleep.
I can lay right there in my bed
Singing and talking to Almighty God as I'm led.

All my Saturdays and off days used to be filled with family
activities
But now I have quiet quality time to read and study God's word
faithfully.
I love this time; there's so much in God's word to learn
It has sparked more hunger and thirst
For Him I continue to yearn.
Yes, I'm thoroughly enjoying this; it took a while to come
But it's finally here
My new, refreshing, and wonderful different kind of
FREEDOM.

April 13, 2013

Welcome

Wherever I am, I want You to be
God, You're always welcome to hang with me.
I love Your presence and Your company
An old hymn comes to mind
"Nearer My God to Thee".

You created us to have fellowship with You
Which requires more than a once-a-week sitting in a pew.
You went often to talk with Adam in the cool of the day,
With Your servant, Moses, You spoke face to face.
Throughout Your word, it's clearly seen
That with Your creation, people, You love communicating.

Oh how special and precious it is to learn
That a close relationship with us is what You yearn.
When any of us neglect giving You that quality time
We hurt ourselves more than we can ever realize.
The void in our lives is there for You to occupy
Only You, and You alone, can permanently satisfy.

I'm so glad I learned how to spend time with You
My heart you drew
With a continuous woo
My mind You blew
My love for You grew
And now, NOTHING else will do.

So, wherever I am, I definitely want You to be
You're ALWAYS welcome to hang with me.
You're welcome once
You're welcome twice
You're welcome, Lord, for the rest of my life.

July 16, 2016

So Glad

I'm so glad to have a wonderful heavenly Father
Who gives me unconditional love
And watches over me from above.
He listens when I need or want to talk
And helps me with my daily walk.
He reminds me of who I am
Wraps me in His loving arms, gently holds my hand.
He never leaves me; He's always there
To show His love; to let me know He cares.
He overwhelms me with His presence and peace
Has welcomed me into His kingdom; His royal family.
He corrects me in such a beautiful way
And still loves me, in spite of my wrongs each day.
He feeds me His word liberally
And showers me with blessings abundantly.
To know that I'm actually wanted by Him
Is very humbling and mind blowin'.

I'm also glad for my big brother, Jesus Christ
Who came to earth, His Father He obeyed
Becoming flesh; for my sins He paid.
Through God's Spirit, he was placed in His earthly mother's womb
He lived, suffered, and died; body placed in a tomb.
He then rose from the grave, as was prophesied
And now at the right hand of the Father, He abides.

Because of all that He endured
I have redemption, salvation, a heavenly home for sure.
Forgiveness, healing, peace, mercy, grace
Freedom, victory, love, and a permanent place.
He's given so much; I owe Him the same
He deserves to be worshipped, for His name to be praised.
Who would go through what He did for all of mankind?
God orchestrated everything and Jesus graciously obliged.

I can't leave out God's Holy Spirit; for Him I'm glad as well.
He comforts me
Counsels me
Teaches me
Helps me
Reveals things to me
Brings things to my remembrance
Bears witness in me of God's truth
For He is the Spirit of truth (John 14:17).
Readily brings discernment to my mind
He's never late; He's always on time.

I'm so glad to have the Holy and original 3 in 1
God the Father, His Spirit, and His Son.
So Glad.

December 14, 2019

For Further Information

If interested in additional copies of this book, please go to Amazon.com

Author's contact information:

Christine Bryant
P. O. Box 262952
Tampa, FL 33685

ms.christine1984@yahoo.com

Made in the USA
Columbia, SC
12 February 2023

11746199R00015